Let's Get Boys Reading and Writing:

An Essential Guide to Raising Boys' Achievement

Contents

OXFORD

UNIVERSITY PRESS

OXFORD
UNIVERSITY PRESS

Great Clarendon Street, Oxford, OX2 6DP,
United Kingdom

Oxford University Press is a department of the University of Oxford.
It furthers the University's objective of excellence in research, scholarship,
and education by publishing worldwide. Oxford is a registered trade mark of
Oxford University Press in the UK and in certain other countries

ISBN: 978-0-19-830376-3

5 7 9 10 8 6 4

Paper used in the production of this book is a natural, recyclable product
made from wood grown in sustainable forests. The manufacturing process
conforms to the environmental regulations of the country of origin.

Printed in Great Britain by Ashford Print Services

Acknowledgements

The Publisher would like to thank Brenda Eisenberg and Jane Penrose for their help in compiling this book.
Character illustrations by Jonatronix Ltd
Project X concept by Rod Theodorou and Emma Lynch
The publisher would like to thank the following for permission to reproduce photographs:
p7 OUP/Brand X Pictures; **p9t** OUP/Ingram; **p9b** Charlie and Anna Clutterbuck; **p11** Marilyn Nieves/iStock; **p16** Violetstar/
Dreamstime; **p18** OUP/Gareth Boden; **p21** K-i-T/Shutterstock; **p22** Rob Marmion/Shutterstock; **p24** Eric Isselée/Shutterstock;
p27 Orange Line Media/Shutterstock; **p31** OUP/Gareth Boden; **p33** OUP/Chris King; **p39** Rarpia/iStock; **p40** OUP/
Gareth Boden; **p42** Digitalskillet/iStock; All other photography © OUP/ MTJ Media.

This Guide has been compiled by:

- Maureen Lewis – **Project X** series editor, independent consultant and author, and leading authority on the motivation and engagement of young learners

- Pippa Doran – Senior Advisor for Kent, co-ordinator of Kent County Council's *Raising Boys' Achievement in English* initiative and author of *Boys Can do Better*

- Karen Young – Advanced Skills Teacher involved in Kent County Council's *Raising Boys' Achievement in English* initiative

Foreword by Gary Wilson – former teacher, now independent consultant, trainer and author of several books and articles on raising boys' achievement

Oxford OWL

For teachers
Helping you with free eBooks, inspirational resources, advice and support

For parents
Helping your child's learning with free eBooks, essential tips and fun activities

www.oxfordowl.co.uk

Foreword – by Gary Wilson

"Boys need to read to succeed" is a phrase I use all the time, yet so many of the boys we are concerned about have negative attitudes towards reading, particularly towards reading fiction.

Through my work with thousands of boys in high schools I would say that less than 20% of boys read for pleasure. The most common reasons they cite for not reading include peer pressure – "It's not cool to read; nobody wants to look like a boff" – and the fact that, "There are more important things to do than read!". Even in primary schools there are countless boys who feel that reading is something only girls do. Why is that?

In part it is because many boys are only ever read to by their mothers or by female teachers. They may never see an adult male reading, and if they do it's more likely to be a newspaper or an instruction manual than a work of fiction. Boys therefore assume that men only need to read to find things out. They hide behind the security of the *Bumper Book of Facts and Figures* because it makes them appear to be competent readers and shy away from fiction because they regard it as some magical mystical thing that only women and female teachers know all about. But the *Bumper Book of Facts and Figures* flicker is not a reflective learner.

We need to encourage boys to read all kinds of material but assuming that the only way to engage and motivate them is through non-fiction and 'fact bites' is to miss the point. Reading fiction helps to counter what is a vital flaw in many boys' learning process – their ability to reflect. It is for this reason above all that I believe we have to shift the stereotypes, raise expectations and engage boys effectively in reading fiction.

Project X provides many of the answers to this problem by offering boy-friendly fiction books, as well as non-fiction. This useful guide supports the series and critically focuses on motivation and engagement by relating to boys' interests and through the use of drama and speaking and listening activities. Its useful strategies for the classroom as well as for the home will ensure that **Project X** makes an extremely valuable contribution to the work of ensuring that boys will succeed – as readers, writers and learners.

Gary Wilson is an independent consultant and author of *Breaking Through the Barriers to Boys' Achievement* published by Network Continuum Press

Boys failing from nursery onwards

Sunday Times 11th December, 1994

Bright girls show up dunce boys

Daily Express 19th October, 1995

The trouble with boys

Sunday Telegraph 21st April, 1996

Girls beat boys at reading – worldwide

Guardian 2nd July, 2003

Failing boys put university drive in doubt

Daily Telegraph 28th August, 2006

Working-class white British boys falling behind everyone else at school

Daily Mail 31st January, 2008

4

Introduction

We've all seen the headlines. Year after year international studies, national test results, research reports and university admission statistics prompt alarming, and often sweeping, statements about boys' underachievement in school.

In reality, the issue of gender differences in achievement is complex. Teachers need to go beyond such headlines and the temptation to accept gender stereotyping. It's not enough to say that 'boys will be boys' or to lament the failures of the 'poor boys'. Instead we must ask searching questions about:

- the evidence for underachievement
- what factors impact on underachievement
- who needs to be involved in addressing underachievement
- what works in preventing underachievement and/or in supporting those who have already fallen behind.

In this Guide we aim to answer such questions in relation to boys and literacy, to provide teachers with proven and practical strategies to help them address the specific needs of boys, and to show how **Project X** can help support boys in becoming effective and engaged readers, writers and wider learners.

We will also explore how understanding and tackling the issues around gendered underachievement is critical to *all* children – girls as well as boys. It is important that a focus on boys' underachievement does not shift attention away from the entitlement of all children to receive the good teaching and learning opportunities that will help them fulfill their potential. So, the good teaching and learning approaches outlined in this Guide and embedded in **Project X** will benefit all children, but will be of particular relevance to underachieving, poorly motivated boys. Similarly, as we read the research, look at the case studies and consider the children in our classes, we must remember that we are talking about *some* boys underachieving, not *all* boys.

The facts about boys' underachievement in literacy

The evidence from national profiling and testing data shows a clear gender gap in attainment in English, from the Foundation Stage through to GCSE. It shows girls performing better than boys and a wider gap for writing than for reading.

The gap starts early. *The Early Years Foundation Stage Profile Attainment* (DfE, 2012) shows the gap between boys and girls continues to be widest in Communication, Language and Literacy, and specifically Writing, where it was 17 percentage points.

The Key Stage 1 and 2 national test results also show gaps in boys and girls achievements in English. These gaps have changed little over the last few years, in spite of all the attention given to the issue. The gap is particularly marked when it comes to boys' writing but the two should not be treated in isolation. Getting boys reading is a step on the road to getting boys writing.

KS1: Percentage achieving level 2+ in English by gender

	2010		2011		2012		2013	
	Reading	Writing	Reading	Writing	Reading	Writing	Reading	Writing
Girls	89	87	89	87	90	88	92	90
Boys	81	76	82	76	84	78	86	80
Gap	8	11	7	11	6	10	6	10

DfE national statistics

KS2: Percentage achieving level 4+ in English by gender

	2010		2011		2012		2013	
	Reading	Writing	Reading	Writing	Reading	Writing	Reading	Writing
Girls	87	79	87	81	90	87	91	88
Boys	84	71	84	75	83	76	84	78
Gap	3	8	3	6	7	11	7	10

DfE national statistics

Boys' attitudes and reading preferences

It is not just in English test scores that boys and girls differ. They also have different attitudes to reading and some of their reading choices are different. Research tells us that:

- Boys are less enthusiastic about reading and less likely to choose to read
  - A survey[1] shows that 21% of nine-year-old boys said they were not interested in books compared with 13% of girls; 46% of boys said they read only if they had to, compared to just 26% of girls.

- Boys are less likely to discuss what they are reading

- Boys spend less time reading[2]
  - 45% of girls reported that they read for enjoyment for more than 30 minutes each day compared to 30% of boys.

- Boys have different reading preferences to girls[3]
  - Boys like reading stories – although a bit less than girls. They prefer fast-paced adventures, mystery, horror and humour. They often enjoy reading series and serials, identifying with a character, a set of characters or a continuing story over many books.
  - They enjoy books which match their 'image' of themselves and this might include stories based around hobbies and interests.
  - Boys tend to have a stronger preference for non-fiction than girls. When provided with a list of genres from which to select, 28% of boys chose non-fiction as one of their top three genres, but only 13% of girls did[4].
  - Boys enjoy visual and multimodal reading opportunities such as comic books, graphic novels, IT and web based reading.

- Reading content can impact on boys' comprehension
  - Research[5] shows that boys' levels of interest in a particular topic appears to directly influence their level of understanding, i.e. interest and motivation boosts boys' engagement with – and subsequent understanding of – a text.

- Boys like to be able to see a purpose in what they do and make links to other learning both in and beyond school[6].

The many and often complex factors that impact on boys' reading are outlined on the following pages but lack of motivation and negative attitudes towards reading are two factors most commonly encountered by teachers – the *'don't'*, *'don't want to'* and *'can but not interested'* readers. A negative circle can develop whereby boys who can't or don't read fall further behind and become even less motivated.

This shows us that **motivation** and **engaging content** have to be given a high priority if we want boys to become engaged readers. As well as ensuring boys *can* read, we have to hook them in to reading and keep them reading.

Why do some boys struggle with reading?

Boys' achievement is influenced by a complex mixture of factors including developmental issues, societal issues and teacher expectations. So there may be many reasons why some boys will struggle with reading and, as a consequence, with writing. Whilst some of the reasons are complex, others are very common and straightforward. Recognizing these problems in individuals at the earliest opportunity will help you tackle the problem before it becomes either embedded or more complex.

Low or stereotyped expectations – Low expectations of boys can become a self-fulfilling prophecy. Sadly, some boys come to school already believing that learning to read is going to be a struggle – a view often reinforced by families, the media and by society. This affects their confidence before they even start school. If a teacher then expects boys to dislike fiction or to find reading boring or hard, some boys will pick up on this attitude and live down to expectations.

Lack of encouragement – Many boys are often initially encouraged to see the value of learning to read but some parents and carers, and often some teachers, believe that once the basics have been learned, that ability will last. The support and encouragement from adults will often dwindle once a child 'can' read. Some boys – even those who started out as 'good readers' – develop problems with reading as they get older because adults are no longer reading with and to them, and encouraging them in this activity.

No reading role models at home – In some households, adults do not read as a leisure activity and there may be few or no books, newspapers or magazines around. Such adults may have had negative experiences in their own schooling, and therefore lack positive associations with reading or the school environment. If a child rarely sees an adult reading – whether for pleasure or for a purpose – then they often fail to develop the notion that reading is an enjoyable or worthwhile activity.

Poor home reading environment – Even those homes that want to promote reading don't always provide a quiet space where children can read without distraction. Some children have computers, CD and DVD players and televisions in their rooms; others might be living in cramped conditions or adverse circumstances. Either way, they may not have a suitable spot where they can spend time reading and enjoying a book. It is important that schools support families in this regard by offering quiet, comfortable reading opportunities during extended school hours, lunchtimes etc.

Macho culture – Outside the classroom, boys can be swamped with images and suggestions that is it 'uncool' to learn and that reading is just for 'geeks, nerds and girls'. To offset these negative connotations, and promote confidence in and about reading, teachers must ensure that inside the classroom boys are only ever exposed to the belief that they will be highly successful readers. There is extensive research[7] on the importance of creating and reinforcing positive attitudes about boys and their learning in class.

The impact of modern media – The huge variety of leisure and entertainment activities available to children these days means that reading can often come bottom of the list. For boys in particular, reading suffers from the fact that it is perceived as providing less immediate rewards than other, more instant forms of entertainment such as films, computer games and the Internet. Another consequence of constant exposure to such media is that some children find it very difficult (and therefore very de-motivating) to focus on decoding a word, phrase or sentence or on sustained reading, because it requires sustained concentration. Reading is therefore perceived to be hard work and not fun!

The view that reading is 'just for school' – Most boys need a context they can relate to before completing a reading task and will not read simply for its own sake. If they fail to see reading as meaningful or interesting to their lives, they will perceive it as something that 'just happens in school'. This turns many boys off reading, particularly those boys with negative thoughts about school in general.

Not enough involvement of children in choice of reading material – Many studies[8] have highlighted the importance of allowing children a say in their choice of reading material, and of respecting those choices – even if they choose books/other materials that are 'too easy' or 'too hard'. Boys find it particularly de-motivating to simply be allocated a reading task and will feel much more committed to read books they helped to choose.

Insufficient guidance on what to read – Many parents, and even some teachers, do not have sufficient background knowledge of the huge variety of fantastic reading material available to children of all ages and abilities. They provide limited or inappropriate resources which in turn limit children's own reading choices and can encourage a negative attitude towards books.

A narrow focus on particular genres – Some boys find it easier to maintain their reading interest by focusing on factual books, often because these books feel more relevant to their lives. However, many teachers and parents will often gravitate towards fiction reading, especially if this is their own preferred genre. Teachers need to offer and promote a wide range of texts. Reading fiction is vital to developing creative thinking, empathy and other skills but too much fiction can put boys off!

Lack of understanding – Some children fail to engage with a text because they have failed to understand it, despite apparently being able to read the words on the page. Lack of understanding makes reading meaningless so building comprehension is vital to building engagement, purpose and pleasure. There is extensive research evidence[9] that reading comprehension can be taught using a range of creative and experiential strategies.

Poor classroom environment – A classroom or school environment that doesn't publicly recognize, enjoy and celebrate reading and writing in all their various forms will not encourage children to do the same. A wealth of ideas for setting up a positive literacy environment is provided on pages 16-22.

Lack of variety in teaching approaches – Boys (and some girls) may not respond well to certain teaching strategies, particularly those tasks which are too open-ended, or which lack variety or pace. Resources which simply rely on visual reading techniques may not be enough to engage them. Children often need kinaesthetic, auditory and dramatic approaches, using games, play, talk, 3D construction and role play, amongst other interactive approaches, to anchor their understanding of and engagement with reading.

Pressures to meet the demands of the curriculum – The pressure on teachers to fit in all the prescribed elements of the National Curriculum means that reading now has to compete for ever-decreasing timetable space. As a result, reading is sometimes squeezed out or, especially for older children, is always linked to a writing activity or work in another subject. It is important for all children to have the time to read – or be read to – for pleasure, as an end in itself. Time for independent reading is also crucial if children are to build reading fluency and stamina, and their own reading tastes, so there are convincing arguments for ensuring it is a regular part of the curriculum.

A whole-school approach to raising boys' achievement

Raising boys' achievement in reading and writing is not something that can stem from a lone teacher in a classroom. Committed teachers are, of course, a key ingredient, but long term success is dependent on a whole-school approach. This means making sure that *all* staff members at all levels – as well as parents, carers and the wider school community – are aware of what is being done to raise the profile of reading in the school, and that all are equally committed to playing their part. It is vital that all teachers act consistently and work as a team to support each other when it comes to the school's attitude towards what boys can achieve, and the techniques employed to ensure that every child fulfils their potential.

In the next section of this Guide we will examine ten key strategies proven to help raise boys' achievement. All of these require a committed, whole-school approach in order to succeed.

So, before looking at the individual strategies and classroom tips, it is important that you reflect on your school situation and think about any overarching changes in attitude or approach that may be needed. Every school situation is different, but here are some questions to get you started:

- How does our school appear to an outsider? Is it a welcoming school where reading and writing are publicly celebrated and valued?

- Does our school have a positive and inclusive attitude to success?

- What expectations does our school have of its pupils? Does our school have any preconceptions about the potential of its pupils to succeed?

- Is boys' achievement a particular issue for our school? If so, is it embedded in to the school development or improvement plan?

- How does our school gather and use assessment data? How can we make better use of the data to inform teaching and learning?

- How does our school involve parents and carers? Does our school have any preconceptions about its parent community?

- How does our school involve the wider community? What could we do more of? What could we do better?

How to get boys reading and writing

A huge amount of research has been carried out on the subject of how to engage boys in their learning. Whilst the results of this research make interesting reading, it is what you as a teacher choose to do with this information that is important.

For example, the research tells us that many boys like competition, short defined tasks with immediate rewards, and being active. So do you construct a curriculum plan which involves boys dashing about, getting lots of prizes and only concentrating on each task for a few minutes? No! This would leave you physically exhausted after just an hour, and involve teaching and learning strategies which are unsustainable – and not always effective.

If boys learn well using those methods then you as a teacher have two tasks:

1. To ensure that your teaching has variety in order to appeal to boys and play to their strengths.

2. To support boys in overcoming the obstacles to their reading and writing, by helping them to concentrate for longer, become better at working as part of a team, and by channeling their more competitive tendencies.

In this section we outline ten strategies that will help you engage and motivate boys and in turn raise their achievements. These strategies, and the accompanying practical tips and case studies, are drawn from a wealth of research and from a successful *Raising Boys' Achievement in English* project run in Kent.

It is important to recognize that every school situation is different, and that not all strategies will work for all teachers or all learners. The important thing is to experiment – and to have fun experimenting! We hope that every teacher will find something on the following pages that works for them and their pupils.

10 TOP TIPS FOR GETTING BOYS READING AND WRITING ...

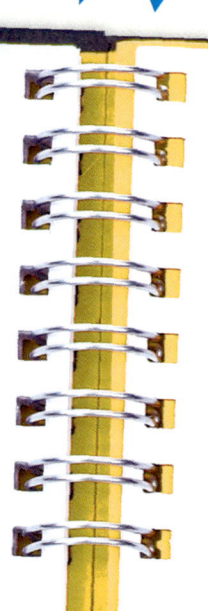

1   Have high expectations of ALL your pupils

2   Create a positive learning environment

3   Make use of reading role models

4   Make effective use of assessment, targets and challenges

5   Don't underestimate the importance of talk

6   Use active teaching and learning strategies, including drama

7   Give them a reason to read — comprehension

8   Use ICT and multimedia

9   Make links between different areas of learning

10 Use parents as partners

1. High expectations

The evidence

It has been shown[10] that a school's attitude towards its pupils' ability to succeed is directly reflected in the success achieved by its pupils. Schools where the common belief held is that all pupils can make progress and do well find, more often than not, that this is what happens. Such schools, and their pupils, do not believe that ability is predetermined or fixed.

Where teachers expect certain children or groups to struggle – for example, special needs children or a minority ethnic group – this is often borne out in reality. The same applies to preconceived ideas of boys' ability. Where teachers expect less of boys because they believe 'boys develop more slowly' or 'boys struggle with reading and writing', the boys tend to achieve less. If a teacher 'gives up' on certain learners, those learners will almost certainly give up on themselves.

It is also important to recognize that the pace of children's progress can vary enormously. Today's emphasis on success is to some extent founded on archaic notions of children being either 'good' at a subject or not. In reality, few children develop in a linear way and often need more time and more opportunity to improve in certain subject areas. This is especially true of boys and reading. So to 'write off' these children is a huge waste of their potential.

It should come as no surprise, then, that of all the strategies outlined on the following pages, having high expectations of all pupils is perhaps the most important – for without high expectations of what learners can achieve, many of the other strategies will not succeed.

What you can do ...

It is crucial for the whole school to emanate a 'can-do' attitude, and to not only have, but show that it has, high expectations of all its pupils:

- Create a positive learning environment (see pages 16-22)

- Try to set aside any preconceptions you may have about boys' willingness or ability to learn – you need to believe that every child has unlimited potential and that the boys in your class *can* achieve great things

- Expect achievement and progress of all pupils – and make sure they know that you expect this of them

- Challenge any stereotypical views held by parents and carers – who may assume, for example, that their boys should prefer science and PE to reading; a parent or carer's attitude to their child's learning is one of the greatest influences on their future success[11] (see pages 38-39)

- Make sure that you explicitly and publicly celebrate learning and learning achievement

- Tackle any 'macho' tendencies to see school as 'uncool' or 'for girls' as early as possible – this may include involving 'cool' male role models (see pages 23-25)

- Set clear rules for acceptable behaviour – and show that you have high expectations for boys' behaviour as well as their learning

- Consciously examine and explore gender stereotypes so that children become aware of how these can limit their potential (see below)

- Make sure you value the things that boys do and like doing – boys often get criticized rather than recognized

- Where boys are reluctant, choose specific strategies to motivate and engage them.

Examining gender stereotypes

Activity 1

Look at a range of print or electronic catalogues that include toys, gifts, books or clothes for children. What do you notice? Talk about the gender issues that these catalogues raise and the stereotypes that they reinforce. Encourage children to discuss whether they agree or disagree with the stereotypes. How do the gender identities portrayed in these catalogues help or hinder children as they are growing up?

With younger learners, you might want to do this activity using birthday cards.

Activity 2

Explore gender stereotypes in traditional tales, e.g. female characters either helpless or wicked; male characters often poor but brave. How do the children feel about these stereotypes? How might they limit people's potential? Encourage a discussion which creates more rounded male and female identities. You may want to write an alternative, modern fairy tale.

With older readers, you may want to select and explore books that go beyond the active boys/passive girls stereotypes. Good examples include *The Turbulent Term of Tyke Tyler* by Gene Kemp, *Bill's New Frock* by Anne Fine, and *The Paper Bag Princess* by Robert Munsch. Many teachers have reported positive and passionate debates arising out of *The Turbulent Term of Tyke Tyler,* and the 'surprise' ending which makes children examine their own beliefs about gender.

Activity 3

Use non-fiction resources to explore men and women who defied gender stereotypes.

2. The Learning Environment

The evidence

The way your school looks plays an important role in broadcasting the school's attitude towards its pupils' achievements – to the pupils, staff, parents and the wider community. It is therefore of great importance that the message being sent out is a positive one. A positive school with high expectations of all learners is a place where boys – and girls – will thrive.

The best schools are vibrant and exciting places to be in from the moment you walk on to the site. This kind of environment has a hugely positive effect on the way children think about their learning and motivates parents to want to get involved. Don't be tempted to use old, leaky or temporary buildings as an excuse for not creating such an environment! Many schools work wonders with low budgets and really grotty buildings.

For boys, creating an environment in which reading and writing are highly valued and celebrated is crucial. But many boys also need to understand that reading and writing is not an 'elitist' sport – it is everyday, everywhere and for everyone.

What you can do ... the whole school

It is important to create a positive learning environment throughout the school – in public spaces such as the entrance, school hall, play areas and library as well as in the classrooms.

- Make sure all staff and pupils feel ownership over the public spaces in the school as well as their own classrooms

- Use displays to reinforce learning and to celebrate achievement – ensure children take an active part in producing them and setting them up

- Make good use of signs and labels throughout the school (see below) and involve children in creating and installing them

- Have a school noticeboard – where staff and pupils can share interesting things they've done, places they've been etc, or where you might display quizzes or mysteries for children to solve (e.g. photos of teachers as babies)

- Use the public spaces to celebrate birthdays or other special personal or local events

- Remember that everything you put up on the walls must reflect how important reading and writing is – labels must be clear, well written and carefully mounted, not dirty, faded or tatty

- Involve children in creating the school learning environment – ask them to contribute ideas and make sure you use their ideas (as well as their labour!)

- Use every possible opportunity to promote reading and literacy – play time, lunch time, PE lessons, assemblies, school fairs, fundraisers, school trips, parents' evenings … and so on

- Exchange ideas with other schools or use organizations like the National Literacy Trust

- Organize school-wide reading events – take part in National Book Week or National Poetry Day; invite in authors, theatre groups or other visitors; involve the local community.

Make sure that reading is everywhere!

Children interact with signs and labels everywhere they go. For boys, this reinforces the idea that reading has a real purpose and is for everyone. If possible, take pupils out to look at the way information is presented in the local community so that they get a sense of reading through signs and symbols as well as words.

The following ideas are aimed at the public areas of a school but can easily be transferred to your classroom.

Activity I

Create labels for as many objects and areas as possible throughout the school so that children learn to read words in context and extend their vocabulary.

Make sure to vary the height and complexity of the labels so that they are accessible to different age groups. Support the words with symbols, and/or include the use of other community languages if appropriate.

Activity 2

Put up reminder signs for everyday tasks and/or to encourage positive behaviour. To make sure that boys don't see these things as 'uncool' you may want to make use of favourite characters or popular male role models to engage children with instructions.

Make use of 'fun' signs and symbols, e.g. 'No entry – children working' or 'Danger – staff room!'

Activity 3

Put up signs in the form of questions or challenges to encourage discussion and interaction with others, e.g. What is the weather like outside? How many people have you smiled at today? What did you do at the weekend?

These signs and challenges will need to be changed regularly so that children continue to engage with them. So why not involve the children in setting the challenges?

Activity 4

Have a school 'walkabout' at the end of each term where pupils can see what other classes have been learning and read and comment on the classroom displays. Visiting classes can leave notes and messages on a board in each classroom.

What you can do ... in your classroom

The classroom reading environment should be stimulating, engaging and ever-changing to reflect the needs and tastes of learners. Above all it should be created with and for the children. This is particularly important for boys who need to believe in the value of reading and writing for themselves, rather than seeing it as something imposed on them by adults.

- Provide a wide range of rich and engaging reading resources (see below)

- Make connections between reading and popular culture beyond school, e.g. favourite films, television programmes, computer games, sports events etc

- Ask children what kind of things they'd like to read – particularly if you're not familiar with the latest popular trends – and ask them to help with the selection of books

- Create colourful displays involving the children in selecting the subject and creating the display (see page 20)

- Create signs and labels for anything and everything in your classroom, making use of character speech bubbles

- Create an area for pupils to display their thoughts and ideas about their reading – their likes and dislikes, recommendations etc

- Display prompts for children's writing – lists of words, character ideas, possible settings, technical vocabulary relating to a topic, sentence starters, questions etc – and encourage children to collect and add more examples of their own

- Put up displays that can be interactive and change daily – e.g. weather charts, word walls, word of the week etc

Provide a rich range of reading resources

Despite the wealth of reading opportunities available today, we still tend to define 'a reader' as someone who reads novels. Sadly, this means that many of us – adults and children alike – do not perceive ourselves to be 'readers' despite a rich diet of magazines, newspapers, non-fiction texts, comics, websites and other media.

In school, many pupils, particularly boys, earn the label 'reluctant reader' because they fail to engage with books and other reading material provided for lessons. They associate reading purely with 'school' and 'learning' and avoid it either because this is perceived as 'uncool' or because they fear failure.

It is important for boys to see themselves as readers, and to understand the purpose and pleasure of reading. This means providing children with a rich range of reading resources and helping them to understand that reading is not just about books, not just about stories, and not just about school and learning.

Activity 1

Every classroom should have a reading corner or a comfortable area where children can explore and freely select reading materials. Make sure you involve the children in choosing resources for the reading area. Try to offer as much of the following as possible:

- Fiction at a range of reading levels, including picture books
- Non-fiction books on a range of topics, including (but not exclusively) topics being studied in class
- Books that link to popular culture outside school
- Comics, annuals and graphic novels
- Magazines, newspapers, leaflets, brochures, catalogues, manuals etc
- Audio books or talking stories
- DVDs – films, documentaries
- Word or reading games.

Activity 2

It is important to encourage the link between reading and writing from the very first years of school. Alongside the reading resources in the book corner, provide a range of writing or mark making materials and opportunities for children to write. Here are just two ideas which can be adapted for use at all levels:

- Have an interactive story strip where children can independently build up a story by adding a sentence or phrase or picture to the story over time. Set different criteria for the story – e.g. must have a happy ending, or must include these characters – and read the final story with the class.
- Provide photographs, illustrations and a range of sentence starters or technical words to encourage children to compose a non-fiction text over time. Pose questions about a topic and encourage children to find answers from their reading.

Create a range of displays with and for the children

Classroom displays are a high profile resource which can engage children in many ways. For boys, displays reinforce areas of learning, provide easy reference tools and can help to celebrate achievement. Make displays bright and interesting and ensure that children take an active part in producing them and setting them up. Draw attention to the displays during teaching and show pupils how they might use the displays to support their own reading and writing.

Activity 1

Create a multi-sensory display with children that will encourage interaction and talk around a topic. Make use of textures, materials and objects that children will not be able to resist touching and exploring. Support reading and writing by including books, letters, magazines or examples of children's own writing or drawing as part of the display. Include labels and questions to prompt discussion.

Activity 2

Put up a display of photographs with captions – this might be photos of pupils' pets, of a class outing, or of a special event in class. Add questions to the display to encourage discussion.

With older children, you may want to assign this activity to a group of pupils and encourage them to create a display about a book they've read, a place they've been or something that interests them. This gives them a purpose and an audience for their work – something boys respond well to – and draws on pupils' own knowledge and interests.

The school library

For pupils who struggle or are disengaged with reading, the school library can be quite a threatening place. These children need to be encouraged to visit and interact with the library and its resources, so it is vital that you create a space that feels both safe and exciting. Here are some ideas for setting up your library:

- Try creating a theme for the library or an area of the library – something that will draw in the boys such as a jungle or castle. Make it an exciting place to be, with lots of displays and posters.

- Have a regular focus within the library to point children in the direction of different types of reading resources – consider topics and genres that will appeal to boys such as transport, hobbies, adventure stories, mysteries, graphic novels, favourite authors/series, new releases and so on.

- Display some books with the covers showing – these are much more inviting than rows of spines.

- Keep the library tidy and well organized – to show that books and reading have value.

- Make the seating area comfortable and inviting. Use smart or speciality chairs, sofas, cushions, bean bags, large bright floor mats. Provide toys and puppets for younger children to share books with.

- Use boys and other reluctant readers as librarians or library monitors. Give them a special area of the library to look after, reflecting their personal interests if possible. Allow older children to monitor the early years' section so they can be 'important' to the younger children.

- You may want to open your library up to the wider community, for example by holding 'songs and rhymes' sessions for mums with pre-school children or by holding storytelling sessions with grandparents.

The content of the library

If you want to engage children with reading you need to provide a wide selection of vibrant, high quality, interesting books and other material that will accommodate all abilities and tastes. As far as your budget allows, make sure you refresh the stock periodically so that old and tatty or dated titles can be discarded and new titles brought in.

Ask pupils to tell you what *they* would like to see in the library, what books would be on their 'wish list' or books they would recommend. Involving children, especially the boys, in choosing books (and respecting their choices) empowers them to see reading as something for them.

Make sure you include picture books, nursery rhymes, comics, annuals, dictionaries, puppets, tapes, puzzle books, games, magazines and reference books alongside the fiction and non-fiction.

You may want to include a parents' section with books, magazines and leaflets on subjects such as good parenting, diet, behaviour management, outings, rainy day ideas, local areas of interest, being a single parent etc. Again, ask parents what topics they would like covered.

If you keep only one literacy magazine in the staff room make it *Books for Keeps*. This excellent publication is full of reading recommendations for children of all ages, interviews with authors, research on reading, advice on setting up author visits and workshops, details of conferences etc.

3. Reading Role Models

The evidence

With primary schools, and many homes, being such 'female' dominated environments it is no surprise that many boys fail to identify reading as a male activity. Most studies into raising boys' achievement place a high value on positive male role models for boys. Even where it is not possible to provide male reading role models, positive reading role models of all kinds are vital for boys. They help to reinforce the place reading has in society, its purpose and value.

Reading mentors in school also have the advantage of giving one-on-one attention to each reader, making them feel more valued than they might otherwise in a whole class or group situation. Specific issues and attitudes can be discussed in an informal and non-threatening way.

Below we explore how different reading role models and/or mentors can be used to inspire boy readers, but first you need to ask yourself the question – Are you a good reading role model?

As a class teacher, do your pupils see you reading during school time? Do you read for pleasure at home? Do you talk to your pupils about your reading? Remember, reading isn't just about novels! You are far more likely to imbue children with a passion for reading if you clearly love reading yourself and demonstrate your enthusiasm explicitly[12]. It will be infectious. Your knowledge of children's literature and other reading materials, as well as of current popular culture (children's favourite games, TV programmes, films etc) also impacts on your ability to select the right books to inspire individual children and develop their reading tastes.

What you can do ...

- Be a reader yourself!

- Find time to read aloud to children – of all ages – as often as possible. Put reading at the heart of your timetable.

- Try to broaden your knowledge of children's literature and popular culture so that you are better able to advise your pupils on 'good stuff to read'

- If possible, use a senior or high-profile member of staff as a reading mentor – this will make children feel important and that their problems are being taken seriously (be aware that in a minority of cases this approach might feel punitive to the child)

- Encourage parents to be good reading role models (see pages 38-39)

- Make use of the wider community – invite in local people to share their stories and to show how reading helps them day to day. Boys respond well to seeing people in 'real jobs', particularly if the job reflects their interests. It helps them see that school has a purpose (see over page)

- Invite in authors to talk about what it is to be a reader and a writer

- Make use of peer mentoring – the opportunity to read with another child, particularly one who has overcome similar obstacles, is an immensely effective strategy for children who struggle with reading.

- Create displays that show favourite characters from books or popular culture reading

- Use 'virtual' role models – making use of celebrity role models to endorse reading is particularly powerful for boys and helps to raise the profile of reading. The National Literacy Trust leads the *Reading Champions* initiative which aims to involve boys and men in creating a reading culture. Resources include an excellent series of posters of famous sports stars reading.

Visiting role models

Before inviting any visitor in to your class, you need to be clear about what you want from them and what you hope the children will get out of the visit. It's best to invite someone in to talk about a topic you are studying as this will make the visit relevant – and if they have a real 'wow' factor job or hobby it will really inspire children's interest, particularly the boys.

Talk to the visitor and find out what they feel comfortable and confident doing. Make sure they are clearly briefed about what to say, including the age of the children and appropriate vocabulary to use, particularly if their role is quite technical. Encourage the visitor to make use of books and reading and to show how these are relevant to what they do.

Prior to the visit, make sure you've agreed exactly what the visitor will do and what they will bring or need – and, of course, ensure you carry out the necessary security checks and any risk assessment.

CASE STUDY:
INCORPORATING A ROLE MODEL

Overview: The class were studying Africa as their focus country during a week-long whole school exploration of 'diversity'. The children had been learning about costumes, schools, homes, geographical features, diversity within the population, traditions, health, language, food and animals and their habitats and were now beginning to look at conservation issues.

The visitor: A local parrot breeder was invited into the class to show the children some African parrots. He discussed issues such as loss of habitat and the illegal capturing and importing of the birds. The live birds provided instant WOW factor and the visitor's knowledge of the related conservation and protection issues was excellent.

On the day: Lots of handling of equipment allowed the children to have a multi-sensory experience coupled with good quality 'talk time'. The visitor brought a large selection of parrot books as well as information such a temperature charts, breeding charts, posters and emails. He discussed the importance of using these resources to support his work with the parrots and how he enjoyed sometimes just reading new books for fun. As briefed, he used the books to model finding answers to some of the children's questions. He then gave the children some questions to research and allowed them to browse the books.

After the visit: The visitor left his books with us as the children had enjoyed them so much. They were well used and prompted much discussion and excitement whenever the children learnt something new.

Visitor lesson plan – exemplar

| **Subject:** Literacy – Speaking and Listening, Reading | **Date:** | **Class:** |

Pre-requisites (from previous teaching/assessment)
Children will be expected to use and apply their skills and learning in a wide range of activities across several areas of the curriculum. Generally the class as a whole has a sound understanding of the following:
- Identify the structure of a book, cover, blurb, index, contents page, title, author, illustrator etc.
- Sequencing events accurately
- Asking pertinent questions to gain more information; locating information in a book
- Understand the need of all living things to be safe and health
- The importance of care of the environment
- Respect of other people and their cultures
- Different ways of recording information.

Lesson objectives
- ☐ To engage in a multi-sensory, interactive, fun activity which will motivate reading.
- ☐ To listen to information given.
- ☐ To ask relevant questions to gain information and understanding.
- ☐ To develop and practice a wider vocabulary in the correct context.
- ☐ To identify and gather facts about parrots through question and answer session with a visitor and his parrots
- ☐ To recognize reading as a life skill but also as a pleasure.
- ☐ To learn from a male role model the importance of learning to read and using books purposefully and for enjoyment.
- ☐ To develop an understanding of the changes in the needs of wild and captive creatures/parrots.
- ☐ To identify some of the environmental issues surrounding habitat destruction, capture of wild creatures.
- ☐ To apply skills previously learnt and link them together in the various curriculum areas, recognizing the importance to many aspects of learning.
- ☐ To share some of their new knowledge with others in the class.

Success criteria
- Foster a developing love of books in the boys reluctant to engage with them.
- Children to have a sound understanding of environmental influences on living creatures.
- A developing respect of other cultures, life forms and habitats.
- Children to have enjoyed their learning experiences and be able to tell me something they have learnt, and something they would like to learn more about.

Key vocabulary
Parrot, Africa, equator, hot, food, healthy, safe, reading, important, ingredients, hygiene, wings, beak, feathers, flight, transport, environment, rainforest, hunted, trapped, cruel, care, extinct, endangered

Differentiation – variation in questioning and vocabulary used; smaller groups for lower ability to allow more individual contact time with visitor.

Resources
- ICT: Video clip of parrots
- Other resources to be provided by visitor

Visitor plan
- ☐ Talk to children in small groups about the parrots and conservation issues, answering questions; look at the food they eat, toys they need, nest box, books, feathers, water spray etc.
- ☐ Talk to the children about the importance of learning to read to be able to find information about the parrots, how to make them better, stopping parrots getting bored, how parrots sleep.
- ☐ Children to have time to handle the resources and books, talk to each other and the visitor.
- ☐ Ask and answer questions. Video clip of training a parrot to do tricks.

Key questions – before, during and after visit
- What do you already know? What do you want to learn? How can we find out about it?
- What is the problem? What can you/we do about it?
- Was it fun?
- How important was reading to the visitor? How did he use reading?
- What did I like about the books I saw?
- What have I learnt today? What would I like to learn more about?
- What did I find easy/difficult?

4. Assessment and targets

The evidence

Effective assessment strategies and clearly defined routes forward are the key ingredients of any successful reading programme. It is important that all staff are fully aware of the school's assessment and 'next steps' strategy so that they can offer consistent advice and support to pupils, other staff and parents throughout the school.

Effective assessment structures are those which help teachers identify the progress being made by children at regular intervals and what the next steps in learning might be. By using this sort of assessment, teachers are able to anticipate when a child, group of children or whole class might need support or extension.

Assessment can seem a daunting subject, but the most effective assessment strategies are often the simplest. As a starting point, you need to have a clear idea of both the school and national expectations of adequate progress in reading and writing at every stage – in order to measure your pupils against these expectations.

But why is assessment and target setting so important for boys? As has already been stated, boys – far more than girls – need to see a clear purpose for their learning. They need to know not just where they are going and what they need to achieve to get there, but why they need to go there at all! Boys also like to see evidence of their progress and find achievement and recognition motivating. Making reading and writing meaningful to boys is therefore crucial, as is setting them clear targets so that they can see the progress they are making. Boys' competitive instincts can be channelled into challenges against their own personal targets and there are many case studies of such approaches showing the importance of challenge and reward in motivating boy readers.

A word of caution!

Whilst quantitative and qualitative analysis of children's progress in reading and writing is vital, it is also important not to use the data to fall back on stereotyped judgements. If the analysis proves, for instance, that boys are doing worse than girls, the temptation to summarize this into a simple gender divide must be avoided. In reality, not all boys will find reading and writing difficult, and not all girls will find it easy. Most successful schools go beyond this simplistic view and recognize the specific needs and the potential of each individual child.

What you can do ...

- If raising boys' achievement in reading and writing is an issue for your school, make sure it is part of the school development/improvement plan – ensure assessment strategies are set up to help you monitor boys' progress

- Combine assessment with quality teaching using a variety of strategies

- Be clear about what you expect each child's learning journey to be, and break the journey down in to the small steps they need to take to make progress

- Assess regularly and in different ways, so that children are always conscious of the progress they are making

- Using books that are finely graded is a good way to track children's progress as it is usually very clear if a child is moving forward or not

- Link assessments to appropriate targets, share these targets with the children and give clear feedback against these targets

- Wherever possible, give immediate feedback against targets – boys in particular benefit from this as an immediate response is a more meaningful one

- Set boys challenges against their own targets and encourage them to self-assess against these targets (see below)

- Use peer assessment to encourage children to talk about what they've learned with their friends – this helps boys feel less 'threatened' by learning and doing well

- Turn reading into a competition as a way of motivating boys (see below)

- Publicly reward achievement and progress using stickers, certificates, characters and so on

- Involve parents where appropriate. (see pages 38-39)

Using competition and challenge

Most boys respond enthusiastically to competitive challenges in the classroom and there are lots of different ways you can introduce competition to motivate boys to read and write.

Activity 1

Give children a *Reading Passport* in which they can collect 'stamps' each time they complete a book. Use the passport to create a learning journey, e.g. you might specify particular books or genres they need to read, as well as giving them space for their own reading explorations. Challenge children to read a certain number of books in a certain period of time, or to visit all the genres. Make sure all types of reading are valued. Reward children on completion of a reading passport.

You could create a similar passport for writing.

Activity 2

Provide quiz sheets which challenge children to find information from books and other resources. Children could work on these individually or in groups, with rewards for those who find all the correct answers.

Activity 3

Involve children in judging books or other reading materials and recommending them for an award. Here's a useful format to follow, which can be adapted according to the needs of the target group.

Define the competition

Judge and select three books for a gold, silver and bronze award. Give reasons for your decisions.

Categories might include, for example:

3 books by the same author, 3 books on a particular topic, 3 books for younger readers

Set up a judging panel

The make up of the judging panel is very important as it defines the purpose and success of the activity.

The panel could be selected by the teacher to target specific children's needs or tastes – or it could be self or peer selecting.

Panels could be large or small groups, pairs or individuals.

Panels could be grouped according to gender, ability, age or other criteria.

Judging

Set the criteria for judging the books and remind children to refer to these criteria when giving reasons for their selections.

Select criteria that focus on an aspect of reading that is an issue, links to an assessment target or simply allows pupils to enjoy reading for its own sake.

Give out prizes!

Hold an awards ceremony with children playing the roles of hosts, authors and illustrators.

Ask children presenting awards to give reasons for their decisions.

Use the event as a literacy opportunity – create invitations, posters, programmes, certificates etc.

Make it as real and as celebratory an experience as possible!

5. The importance of talk

The evidence

Children's oral language skills are crucial to their development as readers and writers. Children who come to school with a rich range of language skills, a wide vocabulary and the confidence to speak and listen to others almost always make good early progress in learning to read. Talk helps all learners to shape and articulate their thoughts, engage with texts, question texts, and gather ideas for writing their own texts. Boys in particular benefit from sharing and reinforcing their thoughts and ideas through talk.

Children's language develops in the early years by having quality oral language interactions with adults. Sadly, some schools today are finding that some children enter school with poor oral language skills. The lack of quality talk in some homes – which may also be compounded by children spending a great deal of time in front of the television or a computer game – has a negative impact on the language development of some young children. Such children need lots of speaking and listening activities to ensure they reach developmental appropriate language goals.

Other children may be at an appropriate stage of language development in their mother tongue but at an earlier developmental stage of English, as this is an additional language for them. These children too will need lots of speaking and listening activities (as well as other supportive teaching and learning approaches) to ensure they experience appropriate spoken language structures and vocabulary.

What you can do ...

Reading can often be perceived as a silent and solitary activity and this turns many children off. Talk helps to make reading meaningful and sociable and can be a very successful way of engaging children, particularly boys. Likewise, reading aloud to children of all ages will help to foster a love of reading.

- Talk can and should be spontaneous, but make sure you also plan speaking and listening opportunities into your teaching, rather than just 'letting them happen'. Have a clear sense of the objectives you want to fulfil from a particular activity and how you want the children to progress

- Try to find or make time to read aloud to children, of all ages, as often as possible – it's an excellent way to help children focus, it's enjoyable and helps them understand what reading is about. It fosters their language development and introduces them to the vocabulary and language structures of written texts.

- If you can't read regularly, provide story tapes, talking stories or other such resources for children to listen to independently – hearing fluent readers read helps build children's own reading fluency

- Invite storytellers in to class

- Make use of puppets in talk with younger children (see pages 32-33)

- Use every opportunity to talk to children and to model conversation – make sure the talk is meaningful and a healthy two-way or group dialogue (let children do more of the talking than you wherever possible)

- Get children to talk about their reading – to reflect on events, talk about characters, predict what might happen next, share information they've learned etc

- Try 'hot seating' a character – real or fictional. Either you or a child 'plays' the character in the hot seat while other children ask questions. This develops skills such as understanding and empathy and is also great fun!

- Use reading partners and reading groups to help children see reading as a social activity – the support of other pupils also helps reluctant readers. Linking up with other classes or other schools electronically can provide additional motivation for boys.

- Encourage parents to talk with their children at home – both generally and about reading. (see pages 38-39)

Activity I

Talk about texts for a purpose.

If you have money to spend on class books or other resources, set up a 'book panel' and encourage children to 'pitch' for a particular book they have read. Purchase those books the class vote for following the pitches.

Set up a lunch time or after school book group. Make this a social as well as a book talk event.

Have a regular 'great read' spot during circle time where any child can talk about anything they have read and enjoyed. Encourage them to talk about out of school reading as well as in school reading.

Activity 2

Set up a 'radio station' and use it as a forum for debates, question time, discussion about books etc. Make use of broadcasting simulations, recordings or podcasts to create a real experience that will engage learners.

6. Active learning and drama

The evidence

Much of the research in to raising boys' achievement tells us that active teaching and learning strategies can have a huge impact on boys. Boys – and in fact most young learners – tend to prefer learning through hands-on activity, exploration and experience and often switch off during direct instruction.

There is a lot of interest in whether individuals have distinct preferences for learning in a particular way and opinion on this remains divided. The reality is that most learners use a range of learning styles – visual, auditory and kinaesthetic – depending on the task, and good teaching usually includes all of these. This adds variety and interest to the teaching and offers learners a range of ways to access a subject. Some children may demonstrate a preferred learning style but it is unhelpful to concentrate solely on one approach. You should ensure that you help children to learn through methods which they may find more difficult, so that they develop other strategies. In life, an auditory learner is not always given the opportunity to learn in an auditory way, so it is important to help children become more flexible in their learning styles, whilst using their preferred techniques to embed difficult concepts.

What you can do ...

For boys in particular, 'doing stuff' makes learning feel real, gives it meaning and purpose and helps them to remember and internalise what they've learned. It is also motivating and enjoyable and can help build children's confidence and self-esteem.

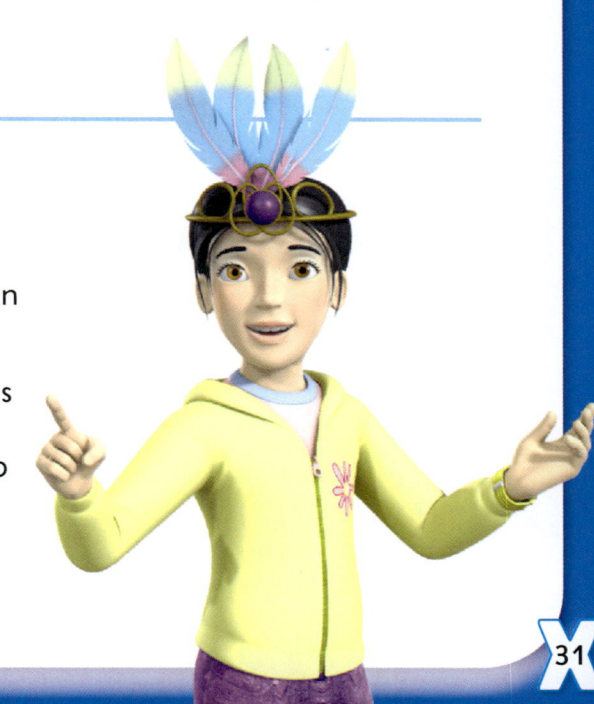

- Build a range of teaching and learning strategies in to your planning, so that the activities are focused and have a clear objective. This will help the children focus too, especially when lessons get lively!

- Make sure you are comfortable and confident in delivering any active learning or drama session with the children.

- Use drama and role play to support children's understanding of a text – this can be done with fiction or non-fiction (see activity ideas below)

- Use drama to explore texts but also as a presentation device, before a real audience if possible (again, this gives the activity a purpose)

- Use small world play figures and vehicles to encourage talk and imaginative play

- Make use of toys and puppets to engage children of all ages (see below)

- Use dressing up and role play to reinforce learning across the curriculum

- Use practical activities as a follow up to reading and/or as a stimulus for writing – e.g. make an object featured in a story, make a mask of a character, try out a recipe or science experiment

- Use themes to inspire the drama, role play and other activities over a period of time – e.g. pirates, myths and legends, travel.

Activity 1

Freeze frames are a great way to support comprehension of a text and can be used with children of all ages. Ask a group of children to read or act out a short scene from a text then 'freeze frame' at a given moment in the story. Use talk to explore what has happened, how the characters might be feeling, and what they might say or do next.

Use this technique with non-fiction to explore information, issues and events.

Activity 2

Invite in a visiting drama or theatre company to demonstrate the value of drama and storytelling and to inspire and excite the children. This fun, multi-sensory, experiential approach can really draw in the reluctant learners. Add to this the fact that the session is not run by the teacher and therefore isn't seen as work!

Activity 3

Use events such as World Book Day or National Poetry Day, or another special day in the life of your school, as an excuse for dressing up as characters from stories or history. It's important that the adults get involved in such events as it adds to the fun and provides role models for the children. Have a specific focus for the day and include celebrations and prizes. Make sure the day is inclusive and involve children in other jobs such as taking photographs/video, creating displays, presenting prizes and so on.

Using puppets

Puppets have been used world wide for centuries to disseminate stories and knowledge to children. They are a powerful tool for teachers because – however simple or sophisticated they are – they weave a magic spell that holds children's attention and can unlock hidden creativity. They are also great for boosting the confidence of learners. For young children, puppets can support emerging language and communication development, but they are equally useful for exploring ideas and issues with older children, helping them to clarify their thinking, learning and reasoning.

- Use puppets to sing songs and rhymes and to retell stories

- You can use a puppet as a 'paired teaching partner' – someone to bounce ideas off and to help you model concepts. The puppet can act as a prompt, reminding you and the children of the things you've been learning.

- Use different puppets with different skills and personalities to support different concepts – such as phonics, vocabulary, spelling, morals etc

- Use puppets as a teacher – some children are reluctant to admit they don't understand something to a teacher, but will talk more openly to a puppet

- Use puppets to 'hot seat' characters

- Use puppets to make mistakes during reading or writing, and encourage the children to put the puppet right – again, children are often more willing to criticise a puppet than a teacher in this role

- Use puppets to ask questions during shared or guided reading – this is also less threatening for some children than being asked by the teacher; 'smart' kids, especially boys, are often reluctant to answer questions that seem obvious or that they know the teacher knows the answer to!

- Provide opportunities for children to play independently with the puppets, retelling stories, sharing information, talking and being imaginative

- Have a special class puppet who goes home with a different child each night, then have a question and answer session with the puppet next morning

- Encourage parents to understand and use the power of puppets.

7. A reason to read – comprehension and book choice

The evidence

Motivation is crucial to the success of most learners, but it is particularly important to boys. Boys need to see a real reason for what they're doing and, unlike many girls, will not do something simply because they are told to. Whilst learning to decode and recognize words are vital skills in learning to read they are not enough on their own – those readers who master these skills, but who lack understanding of what they are reading about or why, will quickly turn off the reading process.

Likewise, empowering boys to make their own choices of reading material – and providing them with the kind of material that will appeal to them – is essential.

What you can do ...

The most important thing you can do as a teacher is to give boys a *reason* to read – and also write. The way that young, inexperienced readers devour books about dinosaurs and can recite their complex names, for example, is evidence of what boys can achieve as readers if they really want to.

- Comprehension of a text is every reader's reason to read so it is important to place a high value on actively engaging children with the meaning of a text

- Comprehension skills need to be taught – you will need to give children of all ages a range of comprehension strategies to help them access a text, and help them to know which strategies to apply when

- Teach comprehension using active strategies such as talk, drama and role play

- Limited vocabulary can be a real barrier to understanding, so it's important to actively broaden children's stock of words through regular speaking and listening, reading aloud, playing with words, collecting words, word games etc

- Provide a range of books and other materials that will appeal to boys – fast-paced, action packed stories, adventure, mystery, humour and a range of engaging non-fiction (further ideas for your book corner or library are provided on pages 21-22)

- Allow boys to occasionally tackle 'harder' texts if they want to – most boys like a challenge and find this motivating (it is a common misconception that all boys want is short, easy chunks of text)

- Involve boys in the choice of books, and respect their choices, so that they feel the reading is for them.

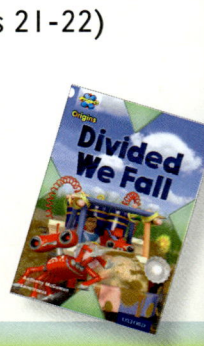

8. Using ICT and multimedia

The evidence

Today's children are growing up in a multimedia world, exposed to a wealth of films, television programmes, cartoons and computer games from a very early age. It would be wrong to dismiss the value of these on-screen texts, many of which are of a high quality and are very sophisticated in terms of their demands on the 'reader'. But there is no doubt that these engaging, action-packed, instant gratification forms of entertainment make books appear pretty dull ... especially to boys.

Children still need to learn to read and enjoy conventional print texts – and much of the advice in this Guide is about encouraging a love of books. But teachers must also recognize, value and develop the specific multimedia reading and writing skills children need to be fully literate in the 21st century[13].

The effective and meaningful use of ICT has been proven to engage and stimulate boys in almost all studies in to raising boys' achievement. There are many reasons for this:

- Most children are used to and comfortable with multimedia texts
- Multimedia texts involve looking and listening as well as reading, so to some children they feel less threatening than books
- Multimedia texts feel relevant to children and provide a link between school and the 'real world' in a way that books, at least for some children, don't
- ICT gives learning a real purpose and a concrete outcome
- ICT offers immediate results
- ICT supports active and interactive learning – taking photos, making videos, creating presentations – and encourages talk, collaboration, problem solving, thinking and planning

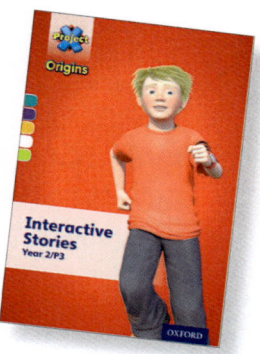

- ICT helps children, particularly boys, overcome their anxieties around presentation of work
- Children rarely lack confidence when using ICT.

What you can do ...

The important thing to remember about ICT and multimedia is that using it simply to 'motivate' the learner is not enough. ICT should be used only where it adds value to the teaching and learning, and where there is a clear purpose and outcome. Don't be tempted to do something 'on screen' when a book or a flip chart will do just as well.

- Use programmable devices such as floor turtles and roamers with young children to support instruction, prediction and sequencing skills
- Use on-screen or audio books to engage readers and to provide models of fluent

reading – such books can be used with the whole class or by children on their own; EAL children in particular can benefit from listening to stories or texts being read

- On-screen versions of books can be effective tools for shared or guided reading, making analysis of a text easier through e.g. highlighting and annotation

- E-books can be a good way to engage readers with texts, and there are an increasing number of children's books available in this format

- Make use of emails as a writing tool with a real purpose – send emails to other pupils, classes, schools, authors, visitors

- Encourage children to email information they find out to others to support ongoing work in class

- Make connections between popular film and television programmes and what children are reading in the classroom

- Use multimedia texts to stimulate talk and writing

- Use ICT tools to support the teaching and learning of writing skills such as editing, redrafting, presenting

- Encourage children to use the Internet – with appropriate security in place – to explore areas of interest to them, as well as those relevant to lessons.

- Teach children to use search engines effectively – including the skills of skimming, scanning and evaluating results

- Teach children how to 'read' a website, using non-linear reading skills, hyperlinks, tracking paths through information etc

- If you feel confident enough, you may want to make use of virtual learning scenarios, online avatars and computer games to support teaching of specific content and skills.

Activity I

Children of all ages can use ICT to create their own texts – these might be books or brochures that they print out, or presentations, web pages, short films etc. Children can use a range of skills such as manipulating text, adding pictures (scanned drawings, digitally created drawings, photos etc), making and adding audio, video or even simple animations. There are a range of excellent hardware and software tools on the market to support this sort of work.

Getting children to work collaboratively on such projects can be very effective and is great for their confidence. Boys love the challenge, without fearing failure.

Activity 2

Many schools make effective use of films and video clips as 'stimulus' material – to prompt discussion or to inspire ideas for writing. But films and documentaries are quality texts in their own right and can be 'read' and studied just like books. There are some great resources, many of them free, available from organizations such as the British Film Institute, Film Education, the Arts Council and Creative Partnerships, and in the children's areas of many TV channel websites.

9. Making links to the wider curriculum

The evidence

Many, though not all, boy learners struggle to make links between different areas of their learning, and to apply skills learned in one context to a different context. This may be as simple as being able to apply decoding skills learned in a phonics session to their reading of a book, or as complex as applying different writing skills to different curriculum subjects. Research also shows that boys in particular benefit from recognizing the relevance of learning to their lives – it's all about purpose!

What you can do ...

Many of the strategies outlined elsewhere in this Guide will help you to embed your teaching more deeply, enabling boys to see the purpose of what they are learning, to enjoy their learning, and to apply this learning more widely. These include:

- Regular and purposeful talk – as a means of teaching and as a way of reflecting on learning
- The use of active and interactive learning strategies such as play, drama, ICT
- The use of learning targets and celebrating achievement
- Involving parents so that learning can be reinforced at home, and made relevant to children's lives outside school

Cross-curricular learning

One way of embedding children's learning, and making it meaningful, is to ensure plenty of practice, repetition and reinforcement of skills in different contexts. A cross-curricular or thematic approach to teaching and learning can support this. It reflects the holistic way that most of us naturally learn outside school and helps boys in particular to develop a wider understanding. It can also be great fun!

- A broad and high interest topic will engage the learner, make the learning feel relevant and can offer different ways in to the learning for different learners.
- Links between different subjects should be meaningful, not forced – you shouldn't be trying to squeeze every subject out of a given theme.
- Careful planning is required to ensure curriculum coverage, but you also need to allow children opportunities to explore a theme for themselves
- A sustained 'block' of learning is essential to support repetition and reinforcement of concepts.
- Make use of the learning environment, displays etc (see pages 16-22) to reinforce your theme.

10. Parents as partners

The evidence

It is well known that parents who regularly read with and to their children, and who act as good reading role models, play a vital part in their children's development as readers. Such parents or carers provide a wide variety of reading materials, talk about books and reading, and demonstrate through their own habits that reading is a meaningful and enjoyable activity. This makes a huge difference to their children, not only in their reading ability but in their *attitude* to reading – something that is especially vital for boys.

Of course, not all home situations fit this ideal and many parents will need the support of teachers and schools if they are to become actively involved in helping their child[14]. Your approach to parents' needs will depend on your individual school situation but it is worth remembering that whatever their circumstances *most* parents really do want to help their children.

What you can do ...

Parents are not trained teachers and, like most of us, cannot remember how they learnt to read and write. In their eagerness to support their child some parents inadvertently create problems for their children and turn them off reading. They may not be good reading models themselves, or they may put too much pressure on their children.

Many primary schools have excellent relationships with parents and carers and guide them to help their children at home, especially in the early stages of learning to read. Such schools:

- Have reading induction meetings where they explain how parents/carers can help with reading

- Role play hearing a child read so that parents know what to expect and what to do

- Provide advice and leaflets for parents from organizations such as the Basic Skills Agency or the National Literacy Trust

- Involve parents in national reading projects such as *Dads and Lads, Reading Champions, Family Learning Week* and so on

- Involve parents and carers in selecting books for the school
- Have an area of the library dedicated to parents and/or encourage parents to come in and share books and reading games with younger children
- Involve parents in celebrating events such as *Children's Book Week, World Book Day* etc
- Run regular book swaps and events for parents.

Of course, in some cases the parents or carers may have literacy problems themselves, or may not speak English as a first language, if at all. This will impact greatly on the support they can offer their child and the confidence they have in doing so. Some schools recognize this issue and put on specific programmes for these parents and carers, both to help their children and to help them develop skills themselves. The direct result of this sort of adult support at a school level is the creation of an improved learning environment for the child at home.

Finally, it's important to encourage parents to maintain their interest in their child's learning beyond the early years. Adult support often tails off sharply once children 'can' read. Parents and carers do not always realize that reading skills can deteriorate – as can attitudes towards reading. Schools should therefore ensure that they encourage parents and carers to continue supporting the reading development of their children throughout their primary school years.

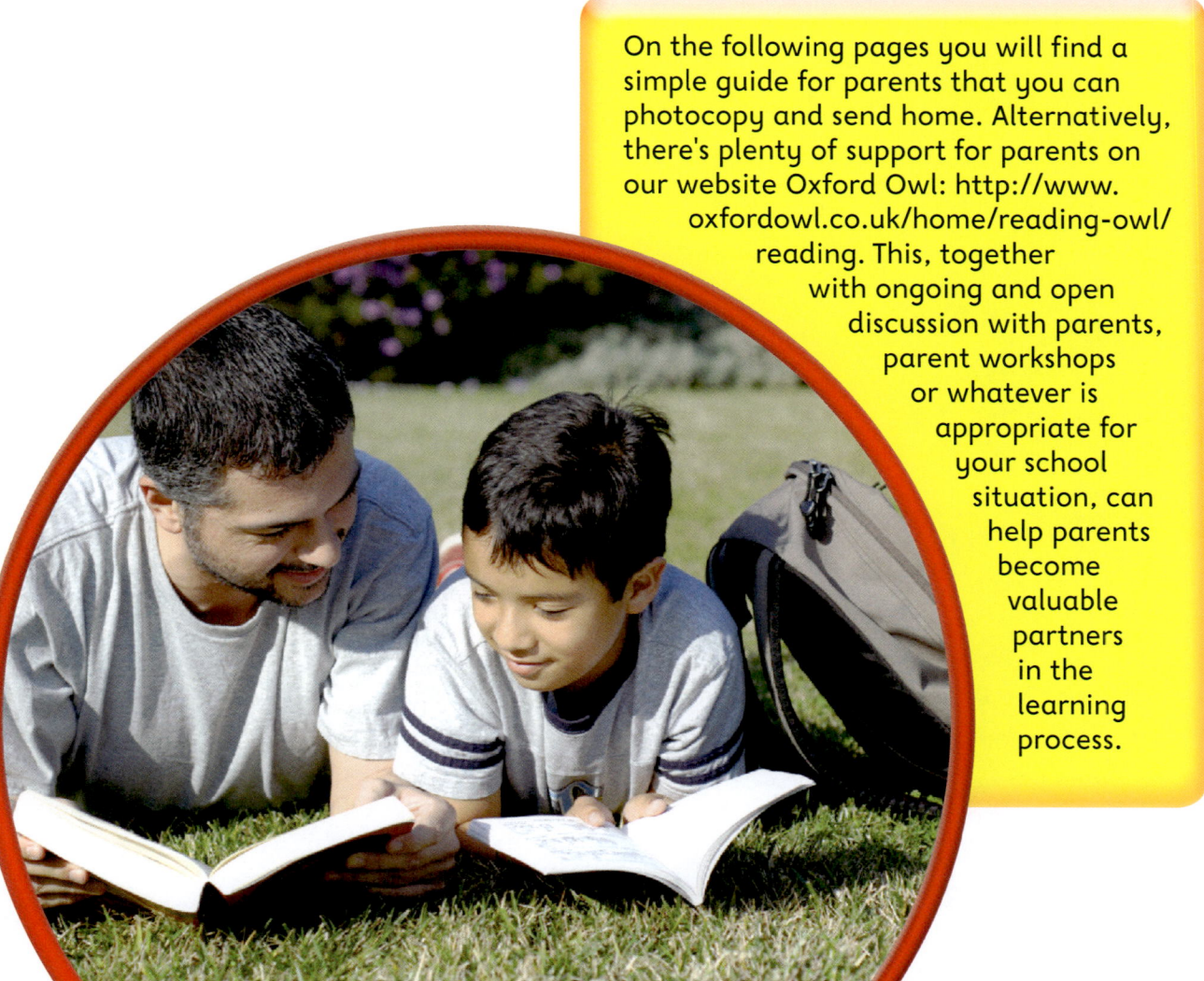

On the following pages you will find a simple guide for parents that you can photocopy and send home. Alternatively, there's plenty of support for parents on our website Oxford Owl: http://www.oxfordowl.co.uk/home/reading-owl/reading. This, together with ongoing and open discussion with parents, parent workshops or whatever is appropriate for your school situation, can help parents become valuable partners in the learning process.

Parents as Partners

Now my child is at school, it's the teacher's job to teach them ... right?

Well, yes ... and no! As a parent you are your child's first and most important teacher. When your child goes to school, you and their teacher become partners in the learning journey of your child. The enthusiasm and interest you show in your child's learning, and the support and encouragement you give them, will have a huge impact on your child's interest in and willingness to learn. This is particularly true of boys.

For many children, and parents, the learning journey is not an easy one. All children are different, learn in different ways and at a different pace. Some children take to reading and writing without apparently needing to be taught; others struggle over every word. Likewise, not all parents feel confident in helping their children, perhaps because of their own poor experiences with school. But all parents *want* to help their child learn ... so this leaflet is for you!

This leaflet is designed to help you:

- Understand the importance of your role in your child's learning
- Overcome some of your own anxieties about learning and school
- Know what to do – and what not to do – to support your child
- Make the learning journey fun!

Finally, remember that your child's teacher is there to help you. If you have any concerns or need advice, talk to the teacher about your child's progress and what you can do to support them at home.

Before school even starts ...

Letters and words are all around us and you may be surprised just how much your child has already learnt to 'read' before they ever look at words in a book. At an early age they learn to recognize shop signs, symbols, pictures, and letters and words associated with their favourite toys, food, people etc. As a parent you can build on this by:

- Pointing out the signs and symbols all around us
- Talking with your child at home and when you're out and about – try to make links between words and objects
- Doing things together that involve you reading – e.g. making food (using a recipe), shopping (using a list), visiting family (reading a map)
- Sharing favourite books or TV programmes together
- Drawing, painting and making things together.

As your child learns the vital skills of reading and writing, the time you spend together sharing books, talking, drawing and making marks on paper (later writing) will help to unlock your child's love of stories, poems, rhymes and information. Crucially, it will help children understand both the pleasure and purpose of reading – and this will help them *want* to learn how to do it. You may also learn some interesting facts about your child's perceptions and interests along the way!

Be a reading role model

Your child is more likely to value reading if they see *you* reading regularly, both for purpose and pleasure. Remember that reading is not just about books and stories – magazines, newspapers, the TV guide, a car manual, recipes, emails, text messages, the back of a cereal packet, posters, letters, street signs … all of this is reading!

Make your home a 'reading' home.

- Have lots of books at home. Go to bookshops or the library with your child. Encourage them to browse and explore books and to make their own selections. Librarians and bookshop staff can also help you.

- Make sure you value books and reading in your home. Give books 'pride of place' in a special corner or box and make them accessible to your child at all times.

- Have lots of other reading material available – magazines, catalogues, newspapers etc – and allow your child to browse them as appropriate.

The importance of talk

Children who talk well read well and write well. That's because talk increases children's vocabulary, helps them to organize their thoughts and encourages them to predict what might be about to happen.

Talking to your child and getting them to talk to you is one of the most important things you can do as a parent – whatever the age of your child.

- Talk to your child as they do daily activities, visit places or people. Talk to them about what they are doing, asking questions and encouraging them to answer in sentences.

- Learn and share nursery rhymes, songs, poems and enjoy saying them together. This encourages your child to have fun with language and to recognize its rhythms and patterns.

- When you read together, talk to your child about what you are reading:
  - ask questions in stories about what might happen next
  - talk about information you find out from books or magazines
  - talk about what is happening in your area using the local paper
  - talk about what's on TV or what's coming to the local cinema.

- With older children:
  - ask them to talk to you about the books they are reading, their favourite stories and characters, the information they have found out etc
  - ask them to tell you about things they've done, what they enjoyed, what they found hard.

- Show an interest and enthusiasm for what your child has to say!

Reading to and with your child – the early years

When your child begins to learn to read they need lots of practice and encouragement. They may bring books home from school to read to you, but will still need you to read books to them.

- Try to read to your child every day – a bedtime story is both enjoyable and settling.

- Children will often ask for the same story over and over again! Don't worry, this is normal and good for developing reading skills. Buy or make story tapes of their favourite books that they can listen to whilst looking at the book, either alone or with you.

- As you read to your child, point to the words on the page. Move your finger under the words as your read them. This will help your child make links between the words on the page and the words you say.

- Before reading a new book with your child, talk about the front cover. Ask questions such as: What do you think the book is about? What characters will we meet in the story? How do you think it will end? What do you know about this topic? What information might we find in this book?

- Look at the 'blurb' on the back cover before reading a book. It will help to confirm the predictions made from the cover and provide information about the content.

- Use appropriate vocabulary when talking about the book, e.g. cover, page, title, author, word, letter, picture, capital letter, full stop, speech marks, question marks, speech bubbles.

If your child is struggling you can encourage them to:

- read the word(s) by saying and blending the letter sounds as much as they can, then help them with the tricky part if needed;

- read at their own pace, pointing under each word if it helps;

- notice if something doesn't make sense and re-read it to put it right;

- build connections between one sentence and another;

- ask their own questions if they don't understand something.

If they continue to struggle, read the word to them. This is perfectly ok and allows them to move on quickly with the story. It's important that they don't lose the flow and the enjoyment of reading.

Above all, make sure that reading is seen as a fun activity, not a chore. If your child is tired or doesn't want to read, don't force it.

Reading to and with your older child

By the age of 7 most children will have mastered the skills of reading and become able and fluent readers. It's easy to assume that they no longer need your support, but they do! This is the point at which children who *can read* sometimes become children who *don't want to* – particularly boys. It is vital that your child maintains their enthusiasm for reading as they progress through primary school, as reading is now the door to all their other learning.

- Encourage your child to share their reading with you and to talk about the books they are reading and what they think of them.

- Continue to read to your child, particularly longer or more challenging stories that they can't yet read themselves.

- Allow your child to read old favourites, even if these books now seem 'too easy' – there's no harm in reading easy things if we enjoy them!

- If you have a shared hobby or interest, look at books, magazines and websites together.

- Encourage your child to develop their own reading tastes and preferences – this might be for a type of book, an author, a series of books, comics, magazines etc.

Conclusions

It will probably strike you as you read this Guide that many of the points made and the strategies suggested apply equally to boys and girls – and you're right. At the heart of raising boys' achievement is, first and foremost, a commitment to good quality teaching, learning and assessment – and good quality teaching, learning and assessment impacts on all children.

This is one answer to the conundrum that, in spite of a continued focus on raising boys' achievement, the attainment gap in reading and writing (as measured by national tests) has broadly remained the same. Boys have made progress, but so too have girls.

In order to close the achievement gap and bring the standard of boys' reading and writing closer to that of girls, we therefore need to do something *additional* to target the boys, as well as ensure good quality teaching and learning for all. This involves:

- Looking at schools with little or no gender gap, comparing practice and seeing if we can identify any changes we need to make in our own practice
- Considering specific boy-friendly strategies and materials to give boys further support and motivation.

Lessons from schools with no gender gap

Ofsted reports and research findings on schools where there is little or no difference in achievement between girls and boys[15] show that these schools share some common characteristics:

- High expectations of all the children
- Avoidance of stereotyping
- Actively examining stereotypes
- Use of active and interactive teaching to involve all children
- Use of formative assessment (AfL).

The avoidance of gender stereotyping and the active examination of stereotyping are achieved in many ways. Of particular note are:

- A whole-school approach around ethos, expectations, rules and accceptable behaviours
- Classroom examination, discussion and thinking about gender constructions and their implications
- A whole curricular approach to examining stereotyping.

Some ideas and activities for examining stereotypes are given in this Guide on page 15.

Boy friendly strategies and materials

If there is still a gender gap, in spite of excellent teaching and learning and assessment, positive steps to develop an inclusive ethos with high expectations and explicit work to examine gender stereotyping, schools often consider further specific boy friendly strategies and materials. This Guide has mentioned many of these but to recap briefly, they include:

- Encouraging lots of talk and social interaction around books and reading, and as a precursor to writing
- Selecting books and other materials that appeal to boys and allowing them a say in the choice of books available
- Using books where boys can 'see' themselves
- Using competition, challenge and reward, sensitively
- Having regular learning reviews, setting clear targets and giving positive feedback linked to the targets
- Using experiential, creative, active and reflective activities to build understanding and engagement
- Using reading purposefully, e.g. having a genuine need or desire to read a non-fiction text
- Providing male role models, reading champions, mentors and reading partners
- Publicly celebrating boys' reading and writing achievements
- Using ICT, multimedia and popular culture texts
- Helping boys to make links between different areas of learning, both in school and in their life beyond school
- Encouraging and engaging family support, particularly involving males if possible.

There are no easy answers to some boys' underachievement in literacy but it is important to their life chances that we continue to offer them the right kinds of support and engaging materials.

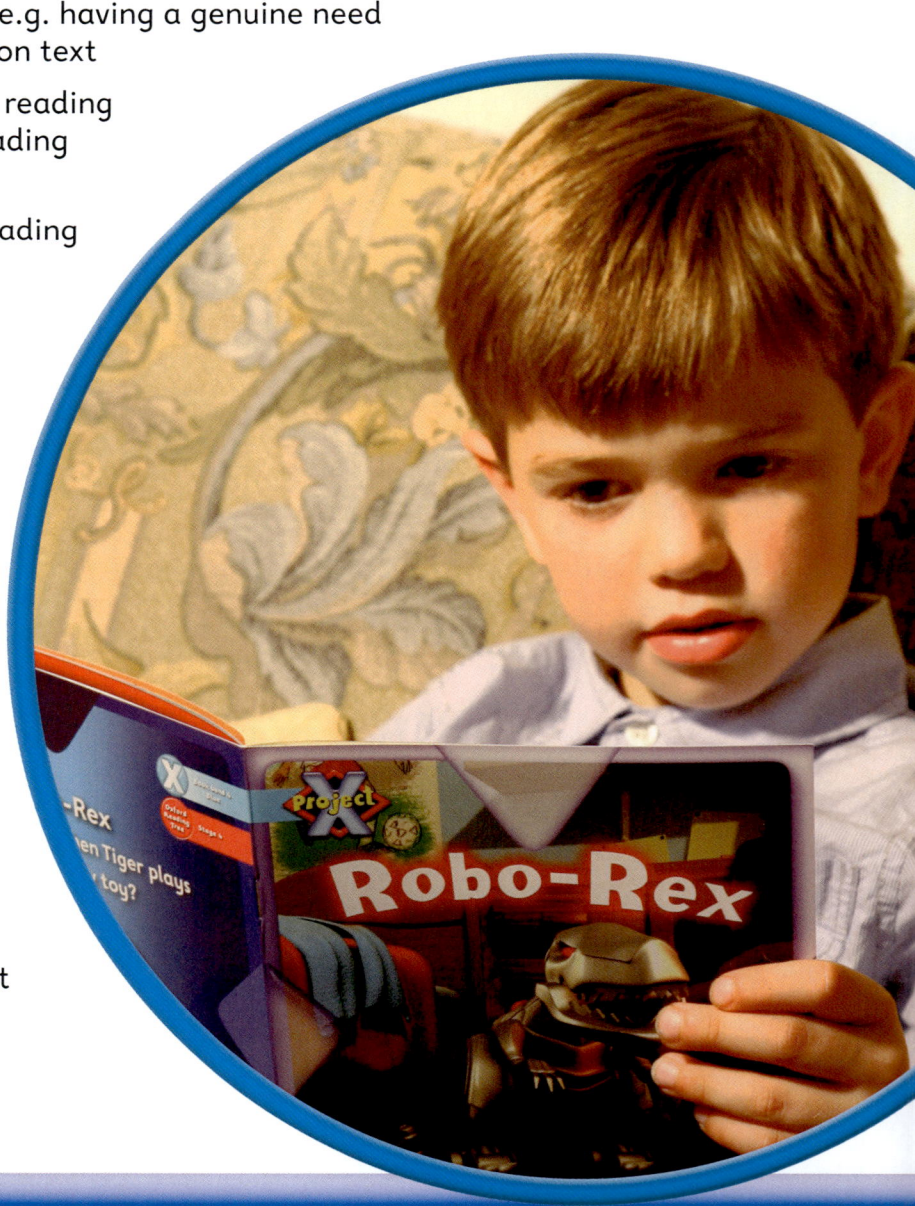

How can Project X Origins help you raise boys' achievement?

Project X Origins builds on all the insights and strategies outlined in this Guide and drawn from research and raising boys' achievement projects. It gives a high priority to motivation, interest and relevance, and supports readers to understand (comprehend) a text and make links in their learning. It does this in several ways:

1 At the heart of **Project X Origins** is an exciting new character adventure, illustrated using modern 3D digital artwork. Recurring characters are a real hook for young readers and the four children in these stories – each with strong personalities – provide opportunities for all readers to 'see' themselves in the texts.

2 As well as providing fantastic individual stories that children will want to read, the character stories contain an overarching 'macro plot' that develops as the series progresses. This exciting adventure – complete with gadgets, vehicles, 'powers', secrets and villains – hooks readers in, making them want to read on to find out more …

3 Across the series the stories are fast-paced and full of action, adventure, humour and fantasy – the genres that we know boys love.

4 Some of the books include 'comic book' and other visual literacy conventions so popular with boy readers. Illustrated episodes, speech bubbles, cliffhangers, character galleries and story maps all help to encourage imaginative talk about the books, which in turn engages the reader.

5 The non-fiction book topics have been chosen to appeal to boy readers and to be both interesting/challenging and accessible – children reading these books will feel that they've learned something new, which is always rewarding. Some of the books feature the 3D fiction characters as guides, to further engage the reader with the content (and not just the pictures!).

6 The thematic structure of the programme is highly motivating – hooking children in to an interesting theme and encouraging them to see how different aspects of a theme link together across fiction and non-fiction.

The **Project X Origins** character story books feature characters that readers will identify with, helping them to 'see' themselves in the adventures. They include strong, brave female characters and boys who, as well as being active, show emotions, value teamwork and friendship, enjoy reading and value learning – thus avoiding gender stereotypes.

As well as engaging content, the approach to learning underpinning **Project X Origins** is active, interactive and experiential. Boys like to learn through such approaches because it makes the learning enjoyable, creative and relevant. What's more, all of these approaches work equally well for girls.

Useful organizations and other resources

Useful organizations

National Literacy Trust	www.literacytrust.org.uk

Reading Connects and Reading Champions are both initiatives run by the NLT.

Booktrust	www.booktrust.org.uk
Booktime	www.booktime.org.uk
United Kingdom Literacy Association (UKLA)	www.ukla.org
The Arts Council	www.artscouncil.org.uk
Creative Partnerships	www.creative-partnerships.com
National Institute of Adult Continuing Education (NIACE)	www.niace.org.uk
Beanstalk	www.beanstalkcharity.org.uk
Speaking of Books	www.speakingofbooks.co.uk
British Film Institute	www.bfi.org.uk
Sport England	www.sportengland.org

Magazines – for book reviews

Books for Keeps	www.booksforkeeps.co.uk/
Carousel	www.carouselguide.co.uk

Literary awards – useful for book recommendations

Greenaway Award	www.carnegiegreenaway.org.uk
Carnegie Prize	www.carnegiegreenaway.org.uk
Costa Children's Book Award	www.costabookawards.com
Red House Children's Book Award	www.redhousechildrensbookaward.co.uk
Blue Peter Book Awards	www.bbc.co.uk/cbbc/shows/blue-peter

Other useful websites

Gary Wilson	www.garywilsonraisingboysachievement.co.uk

Further reading

If you are interested in exploring any of the issues raised in this Guide in more detail, the following books may be useful:

Marsh, J. & Millard, E. (2000), *Literacy and Popular Culture: Using Children's Culture in the Classroom*, London: Paul Chapman Publishing Limited.

Maynard, T. (2002), *Boys and Literacy: Exploring the Issues.* London: Routledge/Falmer

Millard, E. (1997), *Differently Literate: Boys, Girls and the Schooling of Literacy*, London: Falmer Press

Martino, W. & Meyenn, B. (2001), *What about the Boys? Issues of Masculinity in Schools*, Buckingham/Philadelphia: Open University Press

Noble, C. and Bradford, W. (2000), *Getting It Right for Boys ... and Girls.* London: Routledge.

Notes and research reports

1. Clarkson, R. & Betts, H. (2008), *Attitudes to Reading at Ages Nine and Eleven* (Research Summary), National Foundation for Education Research (NFER)

2. Department for Education and Skills (2007), *Gender and Education: The evidence on pupils in England*, HMSO

3. Reynolds, K. (1994), *Contemporary Juvenile Reading Habits*, Roehampton Institute

4. Brooks, G., Cato, V., Fernandes, C. & Tregenza, A. (1996), *The Knowsley Reading Project, Slough:* NFER

5. Oakhill, J. & Petrides, A. (2007), *Sex Differences in the Effects of Interest on Boys' and Girls' Reading Comprehension. British Journal of Psychology*, 98, 223-235

6. Fredricks, J.A., Blumenfeld, P.C. & Paris, A.H. (2004), 'School engagement: *Potential of the concept, state of the evidence*', Review of Educational Research 74(1), pp.59–109

7. Wilson, G. *Breaking Through Barriers to Boys' Achievement – Developing a caring masculinity*, Network Continuum Education, 2006

8. Interesting choice: *The relative importance of choice and interest in reader engagement*, National Literacy Trust

9. Pressley, M. (2000), '*What should comprehension instruction be the instruction of*?' in M.L. Kamil, P.B. Mosenthal, P.D. Pearson, & R. Barr (Eds.), Handbook of Reading Research: Volume III (pp. 545-561), Mahwah NJ: Erlbaum

10. OFSTED (2003), *Yes He Can. Schools where boys write well, Report 505*: www.ofsted.gov.uk

11. Desforges, C. and Abouchaar, A. (2003), *The impact of parental involvement, parental support and family education on pupil achievement and adjustment: A review of literature*, London: HMSO

12. Cremin, T., Bearne, E., Mottram, M., & Goodwin, P. (2008), 'Primary teachers as readers' *English in Education 42* (.1) 1-16

13. UKLA/PNS (2004), *Raising Boys' Achievements In Writing*

14. Sylva, Kathy, Scott, Stephen et al (2008), '*Training parents to help their children read: A randomized controlled trial*', British Journal of Educational Psychology, 28, 435-455

15. DFES (2005), *Raising Boys' Achievement*, by Mike Younger and Molly Warrington, Research Report RR636